The Water of Life
WHISKY

This edition published in 2011 by
SpiceBox™
12171 Horseshoe Way
Richmond, BC Canada
V7A 4V4
First published by SpiceBox™ in 2006

ISBN 10: 1-926567-39-0
ISBN 13: 978-1-926567-39-6

Picture credits: The publishers would like to thank the
Scottish Tourist Board, the National Trust of Scotland,
and the Aberdeen and Grampian Tourist Board, the
Scotch Whisky Association, Gourmet magazine, Seagram
International, John Dewar, Alain Proust/CEPHAS,
Grapharchive and the Corcoran Collection. Every effort
has been made to identify other illustrations. Any errors or
omissions will be corrected in future editions.

Contents

"Loves makes the world go round? Not at all. Whisky makes it go round twice as fast."

COMPTON MACKENZIE, *Whisky Galore.*

THE *Water* OF LIFE

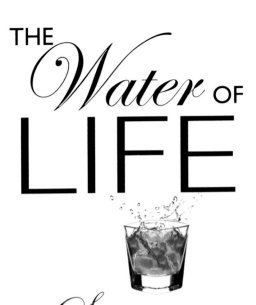

$\mathscr{S}$cotch whisky has become the drink of success, of fashion, of prestige, drunk and appreciated by people of taste and discrimination all over the world.

From humble origins in the hills and in the glens of Scotland, it has become the best-know international drink of all time. A bottle of Scotch is drunk every tenth of a second in the United States of America, a bottle a second in Venezuela, a bottle every twenty seconds in the Philippines.

Each year Scotch whisky earns more than £700 million in the export markets of the world. And yet it remains true to its origins in the remote glens of Scotland, true to the traditions of the patient skill and craftsmanship handed down through the centuries, true to

its name, Uisge Beatha... the water of life."
From Manhattan to Manila, few would take
issue with these proud claims of the Scotch
Whisky Association. Drunk straight or as the
base of a cocktail, whisky is the world's most
distinctive spirit.

As Scotland edges towards a measure of
independence once again, its path on the
international stage has been smoothed by the
worldwide success of its greatest export.

Half-a-century ago, the importance of
whisky was well appreciated as Britain struggled
to recover from the ravages of the Second World
War. Prime Minister Winston Churchill, as
enthusiastic a supporter of whisky as he was
of champagne and cigars, sent a minute to the

Ministry of Food in 1945 with the firm instruction, "On no account reduce the barley for whisky. This takes years to mature and is an invaluable export and dollar producer. Having regard to all our other difficulties about exports, it would be most improvident not to preserve this characteristic British element ascendancy." His wise counsel prevailed and while much of Scotland's whisky production in the immediate post-war years was dedicated to blended whiskies for sale overseas, the global appreciation that followed helped to establish whisky as the universally popular drink it is today.

"Inspiring bold John
Barleycorn!
What dangers thou canst make
us scorn!
Wi'teppeny, we fear nae evil:
Wi' usquabae, we'll
face the devil!"
ROBERT BURNS,
"TAM O'SHANTER"

FACING THE

Devil THE STORY OF
WHISKY

For centuries nature has supplied the Highlands of Scotland with perfect ingredients for making whisky: home-grown barley, unpolluted water from the hill streams, the rich, dark peat of the moors and the granite rocks through which the water filters.

By the 15th century the manufacture of whisky was well established in the Highlands and was already being appreciated in the Lowlands and at Court. An early record reveals that James IV had his favorite tipple, aqua vitae, distilled from barley by a friar.

As demand from the Lowlands grew, so distilleries sprang up along the Highland line to satisfy the growing demand.

The first record of a named whisky dates from 1690. This is the "Ferintosh", from the "ancient brewery of aquavity in Cromarty", the property of the royalist sympathiser Forbes of Culloden. Fifty years later, the Ferintosh "distillery" was sacked by marauding Highlanders, rebels against the English monarchy, who supported the Jacobite leader, Bonnie Prince Charlie. They "destroyed all whiskie pits", a catastrophe immortalized in verse by Robbie Burns:

"Thee, Ferintosh! O sadly lost!
Scotland laments frae coast to coast!
Now colic grips and barkin' hoast.
May kill us a,
For loyal Forbes's chartered boast.
Is ta'en aw!"

In the early 1700s whisky was not the fashionable drink it was destined to become. At that time whisky was thought fitting for "only the most vulgar and fire-loving palates". Even at that stage, however, there were already a few truly fine whiskies to be enjoyed by the discerning, ones such as the "real mountain dew of Glenlivet or Arran, to be offered to guests as sparingly as the finest Maraschino wine".

Politics blighted whisky producers into the first quarter of the 19th century. In 1713 a tax was imposed on malt, a key ingredient in

Glenfinnan, the site of the start of the Jacobite rebellion in 1745 — heralding the sacking of "whiskie pits"

whisky-making and a staple of the Scottish economy.

The Battle of Culloden in 1746, which ended the Jacobite rebellion, opened up the Highlands to the Lowlands and whisky flowed southwards as it never had before.

Following the defeat of Bonnie Prince Charlie, the English government remained

An early Highland whisky still.

vindictive towards the Highlanders. A ban was imposed on small stills where whisky was made and the tax paid on legitimately produced whisky was increased substantially.

But, as Burns later asserted, "Freedom and whisky gang thegither" and illicit private stills sprang up throughout the Highlands, notably in Glenlivet, which was favored for its inaccessibility.

The rights to make whisky became paramount to the Scots and so whisky smuggling came into being. For the next 75 years large quantities of whisky were made in secret and smuggled to hideaways and distant customers under the noses of the "gaugers", the government officers who, supported by the military, tried vainly to stamp out the illegal whisky trade in Scotland.

In the 19th century whisky smuggling was widespread from the Highlands and Islands.

A reward of five pounds for the discovery of an illicit still was turned by the Highlanders to their advantage; when the "worm" of a still, a key part of the apparatus, wore out, the old worm was left as evidence, while the other parts were secreted away to be assembled elsewhere as a working still. The five pounds was a helpful windfall to buy a new worm and start distilling once again!

This game of cat and mouse persisted throughout Scotland until 1823, when distilling under licence was permitted. The first licensed distillery was opened in Glenlivet by George Smith in the same year, making "a greate whiskie", and it is from this small beginning that today's mighty, international industry has grown.

A SMUGGLING
interlude

An official whisky bond house

On one occasion an illicit distiller was warned off by a gauger (government officer), but in a friendly way as both were Highlanders. "Sandy," said the gauger, "you and me are well acquainted and you know I am a man of my word. From now on I am on your trail."

"Thanks," said Sandy, "admit my word is as good as your own and I'll give you a chance. On Friday I'll take a firkin of whisky from Beauly to Inverness on the north road."

Come Friday and the gauger and his excise officers were on that road. A stream of carts of wool, sheep, vegetables and all matter passed by and all were thoroughly searched. Later, a funeral cortege approached, holding up the queue. As it did, a dray of oats pulled out and overtook it in somewhat of a hurry. The excise men chased after it and searched it, all in vain.

In the inn that evening, the gauger chided Sandy for playing a trick on him, assuming that the whisky had been smuggled by another road. But Sandy insisted that he had kept his word and that the whisky was now in Inverness. "Have you witnesses to prove that you took this road?" asked the gauger. "Aye," said Sandy, "there's yourself. You took your hat off to it!"

THE *Warlock* LIQUOR

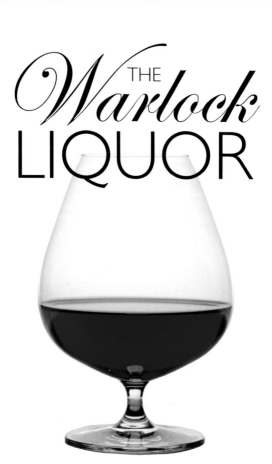

MAKING SCOTCH WHISKY

There are two kinds of Scotch made by two different processes: malt whisky which is made from malted barley only, using the pot still process, and grain whisky which is made by the patent still (or Coffey still) process.

"Whisky . . . the warlock liquor that came to the English out of the mists."
AENEAS MACDONALD,
Writer on Scotch Whisky

16

MALT WHISKY

This has four stages: malting, mashing, fermentation and distillation.

For malting, the barley from which the malt is made is sorted to remove imperfections and then soaked for two or three days in tanks of water known as "steeps".

It is then spread out on the malting floor and allowed to germinate, which can take from eight to 12 days. The barley is turned regularly to control the temperature and rate of germination.

Distilling equipment in today's hi-tech whisky industry

Once dry, the malt is ground in a mill and the "grist", as it is now called, is mixed with hot water in a large circular vessel known as a "mash tun". In this way the soluble starch, produced when the malt germinated, is converted into a sugary liquid known as "wort". This is drawn off leaving the remaining solids to be used as cattle feed.

After cooling, the wort is put into large vessels where it is fermented by the addition of yeast. This takes about 48

Bottling whisky today

hours, during which the wort is converted into crude alcohol, known as "the wash".

The liquid wash is now distilled twice. For this, a large, closed, copper vessel, called the "pot still", is used, in which the wash is heated to the point at which the alcohol in it becomes a vapour.

This vapour rises up the still and passes into the cooling plant, which often takes the form of a coiled copper tube, known as the "worm". The worm is cooled by running water, so that the vaporized alcohol inside condenses and returns to its liquid state, to be collected in the final vessel of the process.

This first distillation, which takes place in the wash still, eliminates the residue of yeast and unfermentable matter in the wash. With their removal, the liquid is distilled a second time, in the "spirit still", to produce malt whisky.

GRAIN WHISKY

Grain whisky differs from malt in that it contains a mixture of unmalted barley and other cereals.

The unmalted cereals are cooked under steam pressure for three hours, agitated by stirrers inside the cooker.

The distillation of grain whisky is a continuous process in the patent, or Coffey, still, named after Aeneas Coffey, an Irish excise man, who perfected it in the early 1800s.

Making whisky in the Coffey still proved to be a far quicker business than using the pot still; whisky distillers suddenly found themselves able to make as much whisky in a week as the pot still had produced in several months.

Now they needed a new market and they found it south of the border where brandy and gin held sway.

Magical MARRIAGES

MALT WHISKIES AND BLENDED WHISKIES

"Lord grant gude luck to 'a the Grants, Likewise eternal bliss: For they should sit among the san'ts That make a dram like this." ANON

The commercial opportunities that opened for whisky producers by the arrival of the Coffey stills led to the inevitable development of blended whiskies. Blends combine grain whiskies from the Coffey still with traditional malt whiskies made in the pot still.

Connoisseurs of whisky invariably head straight for a single malt, the product of a single, named, distillery. Here, the flavors are highly distinctive, the nose highly individual. Within this group there will also be the many variations in taste, color and style, obtained by age and the type of barrel in which the malt whiskies have been stored.

The glens of Killiecrankie — a stone's throw from Blair Athol, home of the famous malt

The alternative is a blended whisky. These are complex marriages of single malt and single grain whiskies.

A blend is the careful and judicious combination of anything from 15 to 50 single whiskies of various ages, compiled by the blender to a highly secret formula.

It is the blender's nose which is the final judge of his creation. He must instinctively know which of the products from over 100 distilleries will produce the harmonious result he is seeking and which will clash.

Following the marriage of the chosen whiskies, they are left in casks for up to six or eight months to harmonize further. After this period, the blender will "nose" the blend and will check its alcohol content to ensure that the blend conforms to the established standard.

When a year appears on the label of a blended whisky, it refers to the youngest whisky in the blend.

THE SIP THAT
Cheers

THE PLEASURES OF WHISKY

"From the bonnie bells of heather
They brewed a drink long-syne,
Was sweeter far than honey,
Was stronger far than wine."
ROBERT LOUIS STEVENSON

Enjoying whisky can be a much more private affair than quaffing champagne or sharing a good claret with dinner. Even when used to propose a toast, and it often is, whisky induces thoughtfulness and occasional melancholy. It is, like a great cognac, something to sip and savor.

There is as much controversy over "to mix or not to mix" as there are whisky drinkers. An old saying is, "There are two things that a Highlander likes naked, and one is malt

whisky" and that is the truth. If asked "What do you want in it?", when offered a single malt, many would urge that the only respectable answer is, "More whisky". Well, not quite. A modest amount of good, still water is deemed acceptable by traditionalists.

However, the huge growth in the popularity of whisky has given rise to an exciting selection of whisky cocktails and other mixed drinks that are enjoyed all over the world.

Many of these originated in America where the term "whisky" often refers to Bourbon whiskey as opposed to Scotch. However, a little experimenting using Scotch will help you find the one that best suits the style of cocktail you prefer. Here are some you may care to try:

Recipes

BENEDICT

Three parts Scotch, one part Bénédictine, ginger ale, a slice of lemon, ice cubes.

BRAINSTORM

One part Scotch, one part Bénédictine, one part dry vermouth, a slice of orange, crushed ice.

EARTHQUAKE

For the adventurous. One third Scotch, one third gin, and one third Anis.

GALLIANO SOUR

One part Scotch, one part Galliano, one part orange juice, caster sugar, half-a-part lemon or lime juice, a slice of orange, ice cubes.

GREEN MIST

One part Scotch, one part Crème de Menthe, the juice of a quarter of a lemon. Serve with a slice of kiwi fruit and a sprig of mint.

MANHATTAN

Three parts whisky, one part sweet vermouth, a cocktail cherry, ice cubes.

MINT JULEP

Large measure of whisky, dash of dark rum, caster sugar to taste, water, crushed ice, fresh mint.

NEW YORKER

Three parts whisky, one part lime juice (fresh if possible), half-a- teaspoon of caster sugar per glass, a dash of grenadine per glass, a twist of orange, crushed ice.

OH, HENRY!

Three parts whisky, half-a-part Bénédictine, six parts ginger ale, a slice of lemon, ice cubes.

PURPLE HEATHER

One part Scotch plus one teaspoon of Cassis. Top up with soda and add ice to taste.

ROB ROY

Equal amounts of Scotch and Italian vermouth plus a dash of Angostura Bitters.

RUSTY NAIL

Two parts Scotch, one part Drambuie, a twist of lemon, ice cubes.

SCOTCH FIZZ

One part Scotch, topped up with chilled champagne and decorated with a single strawberry.

SCOTCH WHISPER

Two glasses of Scotch, two glasses of French vermouth, two glasses of Italian vermouth. Add cracked ice and divide suitably, or, of course, consume it all yourself!

SUMMER SCOTCH

One part Scotch plus three dashes of Crème de Menthe. Add a cube of ice and top up with soda water.

WHISKY MAC

A classic mixture of Scotch and green ginger wine to taste.

WHISKY SOUR

Two parts whisky, one part fresh lemon or lime juice, a teaspoon of sugar per glass, a cocktail cherry, a slice of orange, ice cubes.

WINTER WARMER

Three parts Scotch plus two parts French vermouth. Add a half-part of orange juice and a good sprinkling of nutmeg.

HAIR OF THE DOG

Mix one part Scotch,
one-and-a-half parts double cream and
one-and-a-half parts honey.
Shake with shaved ice and serve.

The value of drinking whisky has long been appreciated for its medicinal properties.

Less well known is the beneficial effect it can have in reviving those who are suffering the "morning-after" effects of an enjoyable, but perhaps over-indulgent, "night before". Ancient Romans, if bitten by a dog, would drink a potion containing a burnt hair taken from the same dog, to ward off any ill-effects.

This cocktail is claimed to have similar properties. The combination of milk and honey helps settle the stomach and restore blood sugar levels.

THE *Spirit* OF THE ORIENT

"Scotch is this island's noblest invention, the only one impossible to fake in Japan, mysteriously unique, at once oily and aflame, wholesome and dangerous, invigorating and numbing, a kind of heather-fed buttermilk gone mad. It is a defier of climates, and time zones."

ALAN BRIEN, *Sunday Times*

The Anglo-Japanese trade balance may look a bit one-sided down the high street, but when it comes to whisky the Scots can hold their heads high. Whisky is the drink in the Orient: the sales figures speak for themselves.

When, in the early 1980s, White Horse developed its first new blend for more than half-a-century, it was targeted directly at the Japanese market. Japanese drinkers like their Scotch heavily on the rocks and awash with water; the new blend had to cope with these local conditions.

It had to satisfy customer demands in other ways, too. Many of Japan's top clubs and drinking establishments are run by ladies with a critical eye for quality. So the new White Horse Extra Fine came in a new, dark bottle (you can't tell when it's half empty), sporting a handsome, dark blue label and closed with a cork that opens with the same squeak of anticipation as a fine cognac.

A couple of years earlier Macallan-Glenlivet decided to release very limited supplies of their 1938 and 1950 whiskies to overseas agents. In Japan, personalized labels were made available for individual customers – a small matter of courtesy and exclusivity for those dipping into their pockets for the 150,000 yen (£300/US$725) that bought one bottle of the 1938.

Not to be left out, ex-patriot communities in the Far East do their bit for whisky exports at a succession of high-ticket, annual get-togethers, where being able to dance nimbly through the intricate steps and moves of Highland dances is the benchmark of social esteem.

In Hong Kong, there is a St Andrew's Ball and a Burn's Night to rival many at home. And in Tokyo, you won't have to look far for some of the finest Scotch east of Edinburgh at the felicitously named Black and White Ball held in October – that's if you are among the favored few to lay your hands on a ticket.

Though other countries produce their own "whisky", Scotch remains the premium drink around the world.

DISTILLERIES OF
Delight

Malt whisky is produced in four principal areas of Scotland: Highland, Lowland, Islay and Campbeltown. There are, of course, other individual distilleries, such as those on the Isles of Orkney and Skye. The greatest concentration is based on the River Spey in the Highlands.

"Glenlivet it has castles three, Drumin, Blairfindy and Deskie, And also one distillery More famous than the castles three."
OLD HIGHLAND RHYME

Each distillery imparts unique qualities to its whisky, and on the following pages the widely appreciated characteristics of some leading brands are revealed.

Highland

BELL'S – Is it Highland or is it not? This leader of blends was started in Perth, but founder Arthur Bell spent a great deal of time visiting and tasting almost every other major distillery.

As the malt from Blair Athol looms large in this blend, Bell's can count as Highland. Even the standard blend states how long it has aged, a ploy to firm up sales in Scotland as, oddly, the United Kingdom's leading blend did not enjoy that position in its home market.

CARDHU – A Speyside Highland single malt, it is also the heart of the famed Johnnie Walker blends.

A fascinating history records how the original owner, John Cumming, illicitly produced whisky from 1811. He was convicted several times, even though his wife managed to convince the excise officers that the agreeable aroma was baking bread.

After the licensing of whisky-making, their daughter built up the business and replaced the old stills. These she sold to a Mr. Grant, who wanted to try his hand in the whisky trade in the nearby Fiddich Glen. Available at 12 years old, it has a nutty and smoky flavour.

CHIVAS REGAL – Here, we are talking marketing, right from the start. The Chivas brothers never owned a distillery, but were up there with the greats of Champagne when it came to blending.

The excellence persists, from the days of the Aberdeen grocery shop where the legend began in the 1840s. They supplied Queen Victoria at Balmoral and were granted a Royal Warrant in 1843.

Originally, they sold the products of others, but in 1870 produced their own blend – in gallon jars. The fruity whisky of Strathisla in Keith is the backbone of their blend. But then add Glenlivet, Glen Grant and up to 30 other whiskies and sit back and enjoy all glorious tastes in a single glass.

CLAYMORE – This has turned out to be one of the more successful blends, produced as a marketing ploy to drain some of the whisky lake of the 1970s. The single malts which form the principal ingredients, Fettercairn and Dalmore, are more than acceptable. But as with much "in-house" champagne, who knows what the blend really is? But its taste says it all and Claymore is one of Britain's top sellers.

CUTTY SARK

BLENDED
SCOTS WHISKY
100% Scotch Whiskies
from Scotland's best Distilleries

IN APPOINTMENT TO HER MAJESTY THE QUEEN
WINE & SPIRIT MERCHANTS
BERRY BROS & RUDD Ltd
ESTABLISHED IN THE XVII CENTURY
3, St JAMES'S STREET, LONDON
40% vol.   e 700 ml
Product of Scotland

Distilled, Blended and
Bottled in Scotland

CUTTY SARK – This is a recent blend, created by renowned wine merchants Berry Bros & Rudd in the 1920s. It is light in both colour and style, with no caramel. Though light in style, it is assumed, but rarely confirmed, that a fair amount of Highland malts are used.

The name was suggested by a Scottish-built clipper, renamed the Cutty Sark when she returned to British waters, in turn inspired by a couplet from Robert Burns's "Tam O'Shanter",

"Whene'r to drink you are inclined
Or Cutty Sarks run in your mind"

The strident yellow label was a printer's error. It should have been a cool cream.

DISTILLERIES OF DELIGHT

DEWAR – John Dewar was the first to sell his blended whisky in a bottle. Hitherto it had been sold in kegs or stoneware jars.

His two sons aggressively marketed their blends at the turn of the century, built the Aberfeldy distillery and gained a Royal Warrant to supply Queen Victoria.

They also, at vast expense, had Thomas Edison make the first "commercial" – a moving picture showing frantic, kilted figures in a painting (below) coming to life. Dewar aim for a full-bodied flavor.

The "Scottishness" of whisky has always been a strong marketing tool. Opposite: the kilted figures in a Dewar advertisement. This page: Scotland's historic buildings are proud to retain their tartan and grandeur.

FAMOUS GROUSE – This is the most popular blend in Scotland, which must tell you something. Made by Matthew Gloag of Perth, it is famous for theuse of older whiskies in its blends. It has a rich, malty sweetness.

GLENFIDDICH – This is the traditional unblended whisky of Scotland, the equivalent of a great château-bottled claret.

The whisky is produced at the three distilleries on the estate from barley to bottle. This is a whisky to be savoured, especially if you can lay your hands on a 50-year-old.

GLENLIVET – This was the first distillery to be registered under the Excise Act of 1823, but it was not for almost 60 years that

George Smith, who founded the distillery, had exclusive use of the name "The Glenlivet", so highly prized was the whisky from this glen.

This is a complex whisky, being made of lightly and strongly peated malt and both hard and soft water. The sherry casks it is aged in add complexity.

GRANT'S – In its distinctive triangular bottle, Grant's successful blends represent the triumph of the family over the problems of the great Whisky Crash in the 1890s, which is why for years their most famous blend was called Standfast. Glenfiddich features largely in their blends, a guarantee of quality.

HOUSE OF LORDS – A blend from the stills of Aberlour and Edradour, originally blended for the American market during the era of prohibition. Blended by William Whitely in the 1920s, who was particularly proud of it. His perseverance in getting supplies through to his American clients made it a firm favorite there and it was regularly served at the White House.

The islanders of Eriskay were the lucky recipients of a quantity of it when the SS Politician ran aground in 1941, a story immortalized in print and on film as *Whisky Galore.*

JOHNNIE WALKER – Johnnie Walker Red Label is the world's best-selling Scotch, with its partner, Black Label, also high up the league.

John Walker was a grocer in Kilmarnock who sold whisky. His son saw the benefit of blends and bought Cardhu on Speyside to provide steady supplies.

The malts from this distillery are still the key to Johnnie Walker labels. There are other rare labels, including Blue, which has some 60-year-old whisky in the blend.

J & B – An international blend from the owners of Knockando and Singleton distilleries. Giacomo Justerini became the partner of George Johnson three years after the Battle of Culloden. Their wine business thrived and Mr Johnson was bought out by the incredibly wealthy Mr Brooks. And so the current company name was formed.

In the 1880s they began creating their own blend of mature whiskies, called Club, which they promoted in France at a time when cognac was scarce.

THE MACALLAN – Here is one of the great Highland malts aged in sherry casks.

The distillery was built in 1824 and taken over in 1892 by Roderick Kemp of Skye. The present chairman, Allan Shiach, is a direct descendant.

ROYAL LOCHNAGAR – John Begg, a distiller of Crathie, on Deeside in Aberdeenshire, made

his fortune after Queen Victoria moved her summer residence to the nearby Balmoral Estate in 1848. She visited the distillery with Prince Albert and her children, awarding it a Royal Warrant soon after (as the extract from John Begg's diary, printed on the label, shows). The blend to watch out for is the Selected Reserve, made from rare old malts.

TALISKER – Set on the Isle of Skye, this distillery was visited by the 18th-century writers, James Boswell and Dr Samuel Johnson, and later by the 19th-century novelist and poet, Sir Walter Scott. Its produce was described by Robert Louis Stevenson as the "king 'o drinks". This is another full-bodied beverage, smoky and spicy.

It is Scotland's natural attributes that give whisky its unique flavor

TEACHER'S – William Teacher started a licensed grocery business in Glasgow, branching out with his "dram shops". He soon became the largest licence holder in the city.

His sons started blending whisky for these outlets, but soon expanded to supplying blends to others. This led to the creation of Highland Cream, which remains one of the world's leading brands.

VAT 69 – One of the oldest brand names, having been blended by William Sanderson of Leith just a decade after the initial experiments into blending light grain and malt whisky undertaken by Andrew Usher in Edinburgh in the early 1850s.

To establish his new, then unnamed blend, William Sanderson tried 100 different blends from the best blenders. He and his friends tasted them and they chose the blend in the vat numbered 69.

WHYTE & MACKAY – Named after two employees of a food warehouse, who organized a management buy-out in 1881. They decided to specialize in whisky, devising their own blend.

This is a smooth, almost gentle tipple, often sold from the large upturned bottles over bars which the company pioneered.

Actor David Niven

Lowland

BALLANTINE'S – From small beginnings in an Edinburgh grocer's shop in the 1820s, this is now one of the world's best-sellers.

Queen Victoria awarded Ballantine's a Royal Warrant in 1895 and after the First World War the company concentrated on breaking Prohibition in America. When this was repealed in 1933, they made greater inroads into the American market, spearheaded by their "first and worst salesman", the actor David Niven.

Their bonded warehouse is guarded by geese, the "Scotch Watch".

GLENKINCHIE – The barley which was produced near Edinburgh was of superb quality and Glenkinchie was founded to capitalize on this in 1825. It is now one of United Distillers' Classic Malts. It is light and slightly sweet. The whisky is a major ingredient of Haig Dimple, in its distinctive bottle, known as "Pinch" in America.

BLACK & WHITE – This is the blend created by James Buchanan and promoted by two twee Scots terriers. His first blend carried his own name and was soft and smooth. It came in a plain black bottle with a white label, which became known colloquially as "Black and White". He changed the name accordingly and went on to supply the House of Commons, as well as being awarded Royal Warrants by Queen Victoria and the Emperor of Japan.

Islay

BOWMORE – Built in 1779 this distillery is now Japanese-owned. It was one of Queen Victoria's favourites and supplies were regularly delivered to Windsor Castle. The award-winning single malts have less peat than typical Islay tipples, but are nonetheless fulsome.

LAGAVULIN – This is one of the great single malt whiskies – powerful and smoky. There has been a distillery on the same spot, on the southern shore of Islay, since 1740. In 1867, it was brought by Peter Mackie, the creator of White Horse whisky, to provide the core malt for his blend, and Lagavulin is still used in White Horse whisky, over a century later.

LAPHROAIG – This is one of the big ones, the equivalent of a major claret. Indeed, many of the words used to describe great wines can easily be applied to it. It is full-blooded, with great depth and has a very distinctive, smoky flavour of peat.

Laphroaig — maker of the world's no.1
Islay malt whisky.
2005 Awarded Best Single Malt in the world.
2007 winner of a Gold Medal - San Francisco
World Spirits Competition.

An enviable task — whisky "quality control"

Campbeltown

ARGYLL — This was the "house" whisky on board the *Queen Elizabeth II* for many years, in the form of Springbank single malt. Nowadays it is a blend including whiskies such as Aberlour.

SPRINGBANK — Full-flavored whiskies are produced here, on the tip of the Mull of Kintyre. The complete whisky-making process is done on site — cutting local peat, malting the barley and so on, up to the bottling. There can be a mild burnt or toasted flavour to add to the smooth elegance of a dram.

SUPERLATIVE SPIRITS

Whisky has recorded some
impressive statistics during its long
history, though few can rival those set
in recent years.

In 1992 a bottle of 50-year-old
Glenfiddich was sold at a charity
auction in Italy for £45,200.

The Shieldhall plant in Glasgow,
owned by United Distillers,
is capable of filling
144 million bottles of
Scotch a year.

"YOU TAK' THE HIGH

Road

... AND I'LL TAK' THE LOW ROAD
AND I'LL BE IN SCOTLAND AFORE YE ..."

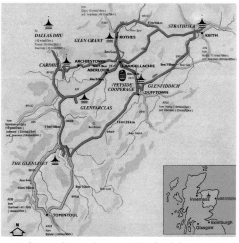

Speyside, in the north-east of Scotland boasts a high concentration of whisky distilleries

"What are the most beautiful words in the English language? I asked the question one day in my *Sunday Times* column and offered bottles of champagne. One comedian, from a highly respectable Hampstead address, sent the following card: Glenfiddich, Glenlivet, Macallan, Glenmorangie, Glenfarclas and Clynelish.' Signed 'John Summerhill (hic)'."
GODFREY SMITH

By far the most enjoyable way to savor this regal drink fully and to appreciate the subtleties of the many varieties of whiskies on offer is to visit the distilleries themselves. Most are found in sublime scenery, hidden away in secluded glens or set against a magnificent backdrop of heather-clad hills and mountains. There is an official Whisky Trail to guide you to almost one hundred distilleries open to the public, where many a visitor succumbs to their charms.

A manageable tour, taking in breathtaking scenery as well as whisky, is to visit Speyside,

...homes of some of the world's greatest malt whiskies

where there is a great concentration of distilleries. Between Inverness and Aberdeen (both about 50 miles/68km to east and west) a circular drive will take you to some of the greatest names in the world of whisky.

THE Malt Trail

If approaching from Inverness on the B9102 your first call will be to Dallas Dhu, the last distillery to be built in the 19th century. It's a Victorian charmer and you can freely walk around.

Further down the same road is Cardhu, the only malt distillery pioneered by a woman. Contributing to the Cardhu 12-year-old malt is the fresh, mountain spring water nearby.

Going anti-clockwise, proceeding south, the next call is Glenfarclas, where five generations of the Grant family have distilled the spirit of Speyside since 1836. Here, you will taste premium malt at its best.

South again on the B9008 takes you to one of the Holy of Holies, The Glenlivet, home of the famous 12-year-old. The vast bonded warehouses take away a little of the rustic charm, but then there's a dram to be savoured, which will improve the view.

From there, head north on the B9009, with Ben Rinnes on your left, and up to Dufftown and Glenfiddich. Still owned by the Grant family, who built it over 100 years ago, this distillery produces the only "château-bottled" malt whisky in the Highlands. Bottling at the distillery, using only a single source of water, gives Glenfiddich its exceptionally pure taste.

Heading north again on the B9014 towards Keith brings you to Strathisla with its oriental-looking twin pagodas. This is the home and heart of Chivas Regal. A free guide book, some complimentary shortbread, and a tutored whisky-nosing precede a superb dram.

From Keith you can go cross-country back to Inverness, or head east for Aberdeen.

Entrance prices vary from distillery to distillery, but invariably there is a full or part refund if a bottle is bought.

GLOSSARY

Blended whisky: Comprising a mixture of up to 50 single malt whiskies (see below), together with grain whiskies.

De luxe blend: Has a higher proportion of older whiskies.

Distillation: Vaporization of alcohol followed by condensation, which takes place twice in the process of whisky-making.

Fermentation: Adding yeast to produce crude alcohol.

Grain whisky: Made from unmalted barley and other cereals by the Coffey still process (see below). Used largely in blended whiskies.

Grist: Malt (see below) crushed for distilling.

Highland malts: Malt whiskies made north of an imaginary line drawn from Dundee in the east of Scotland to Greenock in the west.

Islay malts: Malt whiskies from the island of Islay.

Lowland malts: Malt whiskies made south of Highland malts.

Malt :Barley, or other grain, used in distilling whisky, steeped in water, allowed to germinate and then dried slowly in a kiln.

Malting:: The germination process applied to barley used in making whisky.

Mashing: Ground malt mixed with hot water.

Mash tun: Large circular vessel in which "grist" (see above) is mixed with hot water, to produce "wort" (see below).

Single malt: The product of a single distillery.

Spent lees: The waste residue in the spirit still.

Speyside malts: Malt whiskies made in the valley of the River Spey. A sub-division of Highland malts.

Steeps: Tanks of water in which barley used in malting (see above) is soaked prior to germination.

Still: Distilling apparatus, comprising a closed vessel for heating the substance to be distilled and a spiral tube, or "worm" (see below), for condensing the vapour so produced. Malt whisky is made by means of the "pot still" process. The vessel in which the "wash" (see below) is first distilled is the "wash still", which removes impurities, before the liquid is distilled a second time in the "spirit still", to produce malt whisky. Grain whisky is made by a quicker process in the Coffey, or patent, still, dating from the early 19th century.

Uisge beatha: Gaelic words, meaning "water of life", from which the name "whisky" is derived.

Wash: Crude alcohol produced from cooled "wort" (see below).

Worm: Coiled copper tubing in which vaporized alcohol condenses in distilling.

Wort: Sugary liquid, created in the "mash tun", from the soluble starch produced when the malt germinates.

RECORD JOURNAL

Discover the various characteristics in the whisky for
which each region is known.

Brand: _____

Age: _____

Region: _____

Color / Appearance: _____

Smell: _____

Taste: _____

Sensation: _____

Flavor: _____

Overall experience: _____

Comments: _____

_____

_____

_____

_____

_____

_____

_____

_____

_____

_____

_____

RECORD JOURNAL

Discover the various characteristics in the whisky for which each region is known.

Brand: _____

Age: _____

Region: _____

Color / Appearance: _____

Smell: _____

Taste: _____

Sensation: _____

Flavor: _____

Overall experience: _____

Comments: _____
_____
_____
_____
_____
_____
_____
_____
_____
_____
_____
_____

RECORD JOURNAL

Discover the various characteristics in the whisky for which each region is known.

Brand: _____

Age: _____

Region: _____

Color / Appearance: _____

Smell: _____

Taste: _____

Sensation: _____

Flavor: _____

Overall experience: _____

Comments: _____

_____

_____

_____

_____

_____

_____

_____

_____

_____

_____

_____

_____

RECORD JOURNAL

Discover the various characteristics in the whisky for which each region is known.

Brand: _____

Age: _____

Region: _____

Color / Appearance: _____

Smell: _____

Taste: _____

Sensation: _____

Flavor: _____

Overall experience: _____

Comments: _____

_____

_____

_____

_____

_____

_____

_____

_____

_____

_____

_____

RECORD JOURNAL

Discover the various characteristics in the whisky for which each region is known.

Brand: _____

Age: _____

Region: _____

Color / Appearance: _____

Smell: _____

Taste: _____

Sensation: _____

Flavor: _____

Overall experience: _____

Comments: _____

_____

_____

_____

_____

_____

_____

_____

_____

_____

_____

RECORD JOURNAL

Discover the various characteristics in the whisky for which each region is known.

Brand: _____

Age: _____

Region: _____

Color / Appearance: _____

Smell: _____

Taste: _____

Sensation: _____

Flavor: _____

Overall experience: _____

Comments: _____
_____
_____
_____
_____
_____
_____
_____
_____
_____
_____
_____
_____

RECORD JOURNAL

Discover the various characteristics in the whisky for which each region is known.

Brand: _____

Age: _____

Region: _____

Color / Appearance: _____

Smell: _____

Taste: _____

Sensation: _____

Flavor: _____

Overall experience: _____

Comments: _____

_____

_____

_____

_____

_____

_____

_____

_____

_____

_____

RECORD JOURNAL

Discover the various characteristics in the whisky for which each region is known.

Brand: _____

Age: _____

Region: _____

Color / Appearance: _____

Smell: _____

Taste: _____

Sensation: _____

Flavor: _____

Overall experience: _____

Comments: _____

_____

_____

_____

_____

_____

_____

_____

_____

_____

_____

_____

_____

RECORD JOURNAL

*Discover the various characteristics in the whisky for
which each region is known.*

Brand: _____

Age: _____

Region: _____

Color / Appearance: _____

Smell: _____

Taste: _____

Sensation: _____

Flavor: _____

Overall experience: _____

Comments: _____

_____

_____

_____

_____

_____

_____

_____

_____

_____

_____

_____

RECORD JOURNAL

Discover the various characteristics in the whisky for which each region is known.

Brand: _____

Age: _____

Region: _____

Color / Appearance: _____

Smell: _____

Taste: _____

Sensation: _____

Flavor: _____

Overall experience: _____

Comments: _____

_____

_____

_____

_____

_____

_____

_____

_____

_____

_____

_____

_____

_____

RECORD JOURNAL

Discover the various characteristics in the whisky for which each region is known.

Brand: _____

Age: _____

Region: _____

Color/Appearance: _____

Smell: _____

Taste: _____

Sensation: _____

Flavor: _____

Overall experience: _____

Comments: _____

_____

_____

_____

_____

_____

_____

_____

_____

_____

_____

_____

_____

RECORD JOURNAL

Discover the various characteristics in the whisky for which each region is known.

Brand: _____

Age: _____

Region: _____

Color / Appearance: _____

Smell: _____

Taste: _____

Sensation: _____

Flavor: _____

Overall experience: _____

Comments: _____

_____

_____

_____

_____

_____

_____

_____

_____

_____

RECORD JOURNAL

Discover the various characteristics in the whisky for which each region is known.

Brand: _____

Age: _____

Region: _____

Color / Appearance: _____

Smell: _____

Taste: _____

Sensation: _____

Flavor: _____

Overall experience: _____

Comments: _____

_____

_____

_____

_____

_____

_____

_____

_____

_____

_____

_____

RECORD JOURNAL

Discover the various characteristics in the whisky for which each region is known.

Brand: _____

Age: _____

Region: _____

Color/Appearance: _____

Smell: _____

Taste: _____

Sensation: _____

Flavor: _____

Overall experience: _____

Comments: _____

_____

_____

_____

_____

_____

_____

_____

_____

_____

_____

_____

_____

RECORD JOURNAL

Discover the various characteristics in the whisky for which each region is known.

Brand: _____

Age: _____

Region: _____

Color / Appearance: _____

Smell: _____

Taste: _____

Sensation: _____

Flavor: _____

Overall experience: _____

Comments: _____

_____

_____

_____

_____

_____

_____

_____

_____

_____

_____

_____

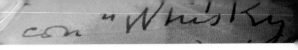

RECORD JOURNAL

*Discover the various characteristics in the whisky for
which each region is known.*

Brand: _____

Age: _____

Region: _____

Color / Appearance: _____

Smell: _____

Taste: _____

Sensation: _____

Flavor: _____

Overall experience: _____

Comments: _____

_____

_____

_____

_____

_____

_____

_____

_____

_____

_____

_____

RECORD JOURNAL

Discover the various characteristics in the whisky for which each region is known.

Brand: _____

Age: _____

Region: _____

Color / Appearance: _____

Smell: _____

Taste: _____

Sensation: _____

Flavor: _____

Overall experience: _____

Comments: _____

_____

_____

_____

_____

_____

_____

_____

_____

_____

_____

_____

RECORD JOURNAL

Discover the various characteristics in the whisky for which each region is known.

Brand: _____

Age: _____

Region: _____

Color / Appearance: _____

Smell: _____

Taste: _____

Sensation: _____

Flavor: _____

Overall experience: _____

Comments: _____

_____

_____

_____

_____

_____

_____

_____

_____

_____

_____

_____

RECORD JOURNAL

Discover the various characteristics in the whisky for which each region is known.

Brand: _____

Age: _____

Region: _____

Color/Appearance: _____

Smell: _____

Taste: _____

Sensation: _____

Flavor: _____

Overall experience: _____

Comments: _____
_____
_____
_____
_____
_____
_____
_____
_____
_____
_____
_____
_____

RECORD JOURNAL

Discover the various characteristics in the whisky for which each region is known.

Brand: _____

Age: _____

Region: _____

Color / Appearance: _____

Smell: _____

Taste: _____

Sensation: _____

Flavor: _____

Overall experience: _____

Comments: _____
_____
_____
_____
_____
_____
_____
_____
_____
_____
_____
_____
_____
_____

RECORD JOURNAL

Discover the various characteristics in the whisky for which each region is known.

Brand: _____

Age: _____

Region: _____

Color / Appearance: _____

Smell: _____

Taste: _____

Sensation: _____

Flavor: _____

Overall experience: _____

Comments: _____

_____

_____

_____

_____

_____

_____

_____

_____

_____

_____

RECORD JOURNAL

Discover the various characteristics in the whisky for which each region is known.

Brand: _____

Age: _____

Region: _____

Color / Appearance: _____

Smell: _____

Taste: _____

Sensation: _____

Flavor: _____

Overall experience: _____

Comments: _____

_____

_____

_____

_____

_____

_____

_____

_____

_____

_____

RECORD JOURNAL

Discover the various characteristics in the whisky for which each region is known.

Brand: _____

Age: _____

Region: _____

Color/Appearance: _____

Smell: _____

Taste: _____

Sensation: _____

Flavor: _____

Overall experience: _____

Comments: _____

_____

_____

RECORD JOURNAL

Discover the various characteristics in the whisky for which each region is known.

Brand: _____

Age: _____

Region: _____

Color / Appearance: _____

Smell: _____

Taste: _____

Sensation: _____

Flavor: _____

Overall experience: _____

Comments: _____

_____

_____

_____

_____

_____

_____

_____

_____

_____

RECORD JOURNAL

Discover the various characteristics in the whisky for which each region is known.

Brand: _____

Age: _____

Region: _____

Color/Appearance: _____

Smell: _____

Taste: _____

Sensation: _____

Flavor: _____

Overall experience: _____

Comments: _____

_____

_____

_____

_____

_____

_____

_____

_____

_____

_____

RECORD JOURNAL

Discover the various characteristics in the whisky for which each region is known.

Brand: _____

Age: _____

Region: _____

Color / Appearance: _____

Smell: _____

Taste: _____

Sensation: _____

Flavor: _____

Overall experience: _____

Comments: _____

_____

_____

_____

_____

_____

_____

_____

_____

_____

_____

RECORD JOURNAL

Discover the various characteristics in the whisky for which each region is known.

Brand: _____

Age: _____

Region: _____

Color/Appearance: _____

Smell: _____

Taste: _____

Sensation: _____

Flavor: _____

Overall experience: _____

Comments: _____

_____

_____

_____

_____

_____

_____

_____

_____

_____

_____

_____

RECORD JOURNAL

Discover the various characteristics in the whisky for which each region is known.

Brand: _____

Age: _____

Region: _____

Color / Appearance: _____

Smell: _____

Taste: _____

Sensation: _____

Flavor: _____

Overall experience: _____

Comments: _____

_____

_____

_____

_____

_____

_____

_____

_____

_____

_____

_____

_____

RECORD JOURNAL

Discover the various characteristics in the whisky for which each region is known.

Brand: _____

Age: _____

Region: _____

Color / Appearance: _____

Smell: _____

Taste: _____

Sensation: _____

Flavor: _____

Overall experience: _____

Comments: _____
_____
_____
_____
_____
_____
_____
_____
_____
_____
_____
_____

RECORD JOURNAL

Discover the various characteristics in the whisky for which each region is known.

Brand: _____

Age: _____

Region: _____

Color/Appearance: _____

Smell: _____

Taste: _____

Sensation: _____

Flavor: _____

Overall experience: _____

Comments: _____

_____

_____

_____

_____

_____

_____

_____

_____

_____

_____

_____

RECORD JOURNAL

Discover the various characteristics in the whisky for which each region is known.

Brand: _____

Age: _____

Region: _____

Color/Appearance: _____

Smell: _____

Taste: _____

Sensation: _____

Flavor: _____

Overall experience: _____

Comments: _____
_____
_____
_____
_____
_____
_____
_____
_____
_____
_____
_____

RECORD JOURNAL

Discover the various characteristics in the whisky for which each region is known.

Brand: _____

Age: _____

Region: _____

Color/Appearance: _____

Smell: _____

Taste: _____

Sensation: _____

Flavor: _____

Overall experience: _____

Comments: _____
_____
_____
_____
_____
_____
_____
_____
_____
_____
_____
_____
_____
_____

RECORD JOURNAL

Discover the various characteristics in the whisky for which each region is known.

Brand: _____

Age: _____

Region: _____

Color / Appearance: _____

Smell: _____

Taste: _____

Sensation: _____

Flavor: _____

Overall experience: _____

Comments: _____

_____

_____

_____

_____

_____

_____

_____

_____

_____

_____

_____

RECORD JOURNAL

Discover the various characteristics in the whisky for which each region is known.

Brand: _____

Age: _____

Region: _____

Color / Appearance: _____

Smell: _____

Taste: _____

Sensation: _____

Flavor: _____

Overall experience: _____

Comments: _____

_____

_____

_____

_____

_____

_____

_____

_____

_____

_____

_____

RECORD JOURNAL

Discover the various characteristics in the whisky for which each region is known.

Brand: _____

Age: _____

Region: _____

Color/Appearance: _____

Smell: _____

Taste: _____

Sensation: _____

Flavor: _____

Overall experience: _____

Comments: _____

_____

_____

_____

_____

_____

_____

_____

_____

_____

_____

RECORD JOURNAL

Discover the various characteristics in the whisky for which each region is known.

Brand: _____

Age: _____

Region: _____

Color / Appearance: _____

Smell: _____

Taste: _____

Sensation: _____

Flavor: _____

Overall experience: _____

Comments: _____

_____

_____

_____

_____

_____

_____

_____

_____

_____

_____

_____

RECORD JOURNAL

Discover the various characteristics in the whisky for which each region is known.

Brand: _____

Age: _____

Region: _____

Color / Appearance: _____

Smell: _____

Taste: _____

Sensation: _____

Flavor: _____

Overall experience: _____

Comments: _____

_____

_____

_____

_____

_____

_____

_____

_____

_____

_____

_____

RECORD JOURNAL

Discover the various characteristics in the whisky for which each region is known.

Brand: _____

Age: _____

Region: _____

Color / Appearance: _____

Smell: _____

Taste: _____

Sensation: _____

Flavor: _____

Overall experience: _____

Comments: _____
_____
_____
_____
_____
_____
_____
_____
_____
_____
_____
_____

RECORD JOURNAL

Discover the various characteristics in the whisky for which each region is known.

Brand: _____

Age: _____

Region: _____

Color / Appearance: _____

Smell: _____

Taste: _____

Sensation: _____

Flavor: _____

Overall experience: _____

Comments: _____

_____

_____

_____

_____

_____

_____

_____

_____

_____

_____

_____

RECORD JOURNAL

Discover the various characteristics in the whisky for which each region is known.

Brand: _____

Age: _____

Region: _____

Color / Appearance: _____

Smell: _____

Taste: _____

Sensation: _____

Flavor: _____

Overall experience: _____

Comments: _____

_____

_____

_____

_____

_____

_____

_____

_____

_____

_____

RECORD JOURNAL

Discover the various characteristics in the whisky for which each region is known.

Brand: _____

Age: _____

Region: _____

Color / Appearance: _____

Smell: _____

Taste: _____

Sensation: _____

Flavor: _____

Overall experience: _____

Comments: _____

_____

_____

_____

_____

_____

_____

_____

_____

_____

_____

_____

RECORD JOURNAL

Discover the various characteristics in the whisky for which each region is known.

Brand: _____

Age: _____

Region: _____

Color / Appearance: _____

Smell: _____

Taste: _____

Sensation: _____

Flavor: _____

Overall experience: _____

Comments: _____
_____
_____
_____
_____
_____
_____
_____
_____
_____
_____
_____

con "Whisky

RECORD JOURNAL

Discover the various characteristics in the whisky for which each region is known.

Brand: _____

Age: _____

Region: _____

Color / Appearance: _____

Smell: _____

Taste: _____

Sensation: _____

Flavor: _____

Overall experience: _____

Comments: _____

_____

_____

_____

_____

_____

_____

_____

_____

_____

_____

_____

_____

RECORD JOURNAL

Discover the various characteristics in the whisky for which each region is known.

Brand: _____

Age: _____

Region: _____

Color / Appearance: _____

Smell: _____

Taste: _____

Sensation: _____

Flavor: _____

Overall experience: _____

Comments: _____

_____

_____

_____

_____

_____

_____

_____

_____

_____

_____

RECORD JOURNAL

Discover the various characteristics in the whisky for which each region is known.

Brand: _____

Age: _____

Region: _____

Color / Appearance: _____

Smell: _____

Taste: _____

Sensation: _____

Flavor: _____

Overall experience: _____

Comments: _____

_____

_____

_____

_____

_____

_____

_____

_____

_____

_____

RECORD JOURNAL

Discover the various characteristics in the whisky for which each region is known.

Brand: _____

Age: _____

Region: _____

Color / Appearance: _____

Smell: _____

Taste: _____

Sensation: _____

Flavor: _____

Overall experience: _____

Comments: _____

_____

_____

_____

_____

_____

_____

_____

_____

_____

_____

RECORD JOURNAL

Discover the various characteristics in the whisky for which each region is known.

Brand: _____

Age: _____

Region: _____

Color / Appearance: _____

Smell: _____

Taste: _____

Sensation: _____

Flavor: _____

Overall experience: _____

Comments: _____
_____
_____
_____
_____
_____
_____
_____
_____
_____
_____
_____
_____

RECORD JOURNAL

Discover the various characteristics in the whisky for which each region is known.

Brand: _____

Age: _____

Region: _____

Color / Appearance: _____

Smell: _____

Taste: _____

Sensation: _____

Flavor: _____

Overall experience: _____

Comments: _____
_____
_____
_____
_____
_____
_____
_____
_____
_____
_____
_____
_____
_____

RECORD JOURNAL

Discover the various characteristics in the whisky for which each region is known.

Brand: _____

Age: _____

Region: _____

Color / Appearance: _____

Smell: _____

Taste: _____

Sensation: _____

Flavor: _____

Overall experience: _____

Comments: _____
_____
_____
_____
_____
_____
_____
_____
_____
_____
_____
_____
_____

RECORD JOURNAL

Discover the various characteristics in the whisky for which each region is known.

Brand: _____

Age: _____

Region: _____

Color / Appearance: _____

Smell: _____

Taste: _____

Sensation: _____

Flavor: _____

Overall experience: _____

Comments: _____
_____
_____
_____
_____
_____
_____
_____
_____
_____
_____
_____
_____
_____

RECORD JOURNAL

Discover the various characteristics in the whisky for which each region is known.

Brand: _____

Age: _____

Region: _____

Color / Appearance: _____

Smell: _____

Taste: _____

Sensation: _____

Flavor: _____

Overall experience: _____

Comments: _____

_____

_____

_____

_____

_____

_____

_____

_____

_____

_____

RECORD JOURNAL

Discover the various characteristics in the whisky for which each region is known.

Brand: _____

Age: _____

Region: _____

Color / Appearance: _____

Smell: _____

Taste: _____

Sensation: _____

Flavor: _____

Overall experience: _____

Comments: _____

_____
_____
_____
_____
_____
_____
_____
_____
_____
_____
_____
_____

RECORD JOURNAL

Discover the various characteristics in the whisky for which each region is known.

Brand: _____

Age: _____

Region: _____

Color / Appearance: _____

Smell: _____

Taste: _____

Sensation: _____

Flavor: _____

Overall experience: _____

Comments: _____
_____
_____
_____
_____
_____
_____
_____
_____
_____
_____
_____

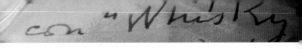

RECORD JOURNAL

Discover the various characteristics in the whisky for which each region is known.

Brand: _____

Age: _____

Region: _____

Color / Appearance: _____

Smell: _____

Taste: _____

Sensation: _____

Flavor: _____

Overall experience: _____

Comments: _____

_____

_____

_____

_____

_____

_____

_____

_____

_____

_____

_____

RECORD JOURNAL

Discover the various characteristics in the whisky for which each region is known.

Brand: _____

Age: _____

Region: _____

Color/Appearance: _____

Smell: _____

Taste: _____

Sensation: _____

Flavor: _____

Overall experience: _____

Comments: _____
_____
_____
_____
_____
_____
_____
_____
_____
_____
_____
_____
_____

A CUP OF KINDNESS

"Should auld acquaintance be forgot,
And never brought to mind?
Should auld acquaintance be forgot,
And days o auld lang syne?
For auld lang syne my Dear,
For auld lang syne,
We'll tak a cup o kindness yet,
For auld lang syne."
ROBERT BURNS